I can write
a book
series

I can write a book about

Butterflies

Bobbie Kalman
Crabtree Publishing Company
www.crabtreebooks.com

Created by Bobbie Kalman

Dedicated by Samantha Crabtree
For my beautiful Melia Diamond Embry
I love you very much and wish I could see you more often.

**Author and
Editor-in-Chief**
Bobbie Kalman

Editors
Kathy Middleton
Crystal Sikkens

Photo research
Bobbie Kalman

Design
Bobbie Kalman
Katherine Berti
Samantha Crabtree
 (logo and cover)

Prepress technician
Katherine Berti

Print and production coordinator
Katherine Berti

Illustrations
Barbara Bedell: p. 12 (arrows),
 29 (arrows), 29 (green caterpillar)
Antoinette "Cookie" Bortolon:
 p. 9 (monarch butterflies)
Margaret Amy Salter: p. 12 (center
 right [hatching])
Tiffany Wybouw: p. 22 (jars)

Photographs
Dreamstime: p. 10 (bottom right)
Bobbie Kalman: back cover inset,
 p. 5 (top center inset), 15 (center
 right inset), 18 (bottom left inset),
 25 (top right)
Shutterstock: cover, logo, title page,
 p. 3, 4, 5 (all except top center
 inset), 6, 8, 9 (all except monarch
 butterflies), 10 (center and bottom
 left), 11, 12 (all except arrows and
 hatching), 13, 14, 15 (all except
 center right inset), 16, 17, 18 (all
 except bottom left inset), 19, 20, 21,
 22 (mature monarch), 23, 24, 25 (top
 left and bottom), 26, 27, 28, 29, 30

Library and Archives Canada Cataloguing in Publication

Kalman, Bobbie
 I can write a book about butterflies / Bobbie Kalman.

(I can write a book series)
Includes index.
Issued also in electronic format.
ISBN 978-0-7787-7987-2 (bound).--ISBN 978-0-7787-7996-4 (pbk.)

 1. Butterflies--Juvenile literature. 2. Biology--Authorship--
Juvenile literature. 3. Composition (Language arts)--Juvenile
literature. 4. English language--Composition and exercises--
Juvenile literature. 5. Book design--Juvenile literature. I. Title.
II. Series: Kalman, Bobbie. I can write a book.

QL544.2.K337 2012   j595.78'9   C2012-901152-5

Library of Congress Cataloging-in-Publication Data

Kalman, Bobbie.
 I can write a book about butterflies / Bobbie Kalman.
  p. cm.-- (I can write a book series)
 Includes index.
 ISBN 978-0-7787-7987-2 (reinforced library binding : alk. paper) -- ISBN 978-0-
7787-7996-4 (pbk. : alk. paper) -- ISBN 978-1-4271-7878-7 (electronic pdf) -- ISBN
978-1-4271-7993-7 (electronic html)
1. Butterflies--Juvenile literature. 2. Creative writing--Juvenile literature. I.
Title.

QL544.2.K35175 2012
595.78'9--dc23
                                                     2012005751

Crabtree Publishing Company

www.crabtreebooks.com   1-800-387-7650

Printed in Canada/042012/KR20120316

**Published in Canada
Crabtree Publishing**
616 Welland Ave.
St. Catharines, Ontario
L2M 5V6

**Published in the United States
Crabtree Publishing**
PMB 59051
350 Fifth Avenue, 59th Floor
New York, New York 10118

**Published in the United Kingdom
Crabtree Publishing**
Maritime House
Basin Road North, Hove
BN41 1WR

**Published in Australia
Crabtree Publishing**
3 Charles Street
Coburg North
VIC 3058

Table of contents

A book about butterflies

There are two kinds of books. **Fiction** books are stories written from someone's imagination. **Non-fiction** books are true. They can contain facts about animals, habitats, countries, history, and many more subjects. They can also be true stories about real people. This non-fiction book shows you how to write and **publish** a non-fiction book about butterflies. To publish is to share the final copy of your work with others. What would you like to write about butterflies?

Bobbie's blog

Before I was an **author**, I was a teacher. Now I teach through my books. I love butterflies and have written many books about them. Writing books about butterflies is fun. I will help you write a book so you can become an author, as well as a teacher.

When you write a book, you become an author. When you publish a book, you share it with others and become a teacher, too.

You can write your own book or write one with some friends. They can become your writing team.

Parts of a book

Have you written reports for school? Writing a non-fiction book is like writing a report, but there are more parts and pages to a book. A book's pages are held together by a **cover**. A cover is the outside of the book. It is the first part of a book that people see. The front cover of a book tells you the title of the book and the author's name. The back cover may tell you what the book is about or include other books written by the author. It will also have the name of the **publisher** and the price of the book. The book's **spine** is what you see when the book is sitting on a shelf. It contains the book's title and the names of the author and publisher.

back cover   *spine*   *front cover*

The title page

The first page of a book is called the **title page**. The picture on the right shows the title page of this book. What information does it give you?

Copyright page

The second page in this book is the **copyright** page. Copyright means that people cannot copy all or parts of the book without the author's or publisher's permission. The copyright page also gives you the following information:

- the names of the people who helped publish this book
- the addresses of the publisher
- a **dedication**, or the words used to honor someone by placing his or her name in the book
- the **cataloging information**, a section of the book that tells the author's name, the title of the book, the year the book was published, and what kind of book it is

Contents, glossary, index

The **table of contents** tells you what the **chapters** are in the book and on which pages they begin. The **glossary** is a small dictionary that explains special words used in the book. The **index** is an ABC list of the topics with the page numbers of where they are in the book.

I can write a book about **Butterflies**

Bobbie Kalman
Crabtree Publishing Company
www.crabtreebooks.com

The top picture shows the title page, and the bottom shows the table of contents of this book.

Table of contents

Big ideas about butterflies

Non-fiction books teach **big ideas**, or important topics, about a subject. When you write a book about butterflies, there are several big ideas you can explore. Some of these big ideas are shown here. You can choose to research and write about them all, or you can pick one idea and write about it in more detail.

Insect bodies

Insects are animals with three body parts, six legs, and no backbones. How do butterflies use their insect body parts to stay alive?

Butterfly symmetry

Butterflies have **symmetry**. Write about symmetry in butterflies and other animals.

Symmetry means two sides of something are the same.

Metamorphosis

A butterfly's **life cycle** includes big changes called **metamorphosis**. Write about these changes.

egg

caterpillar

pupa

adult butterfly

Butterfly migration

Some butterflies **migrate**, or fly far away to warm places for winter. Write about monarch migration.

Monarch butterflies fly to Mexico for the winter.

Pollen is the powder found in flowers.

Pollination

Plants need **pollen** to make new plants. Write about how butterflies help plants grow when they fly from flower to flower.

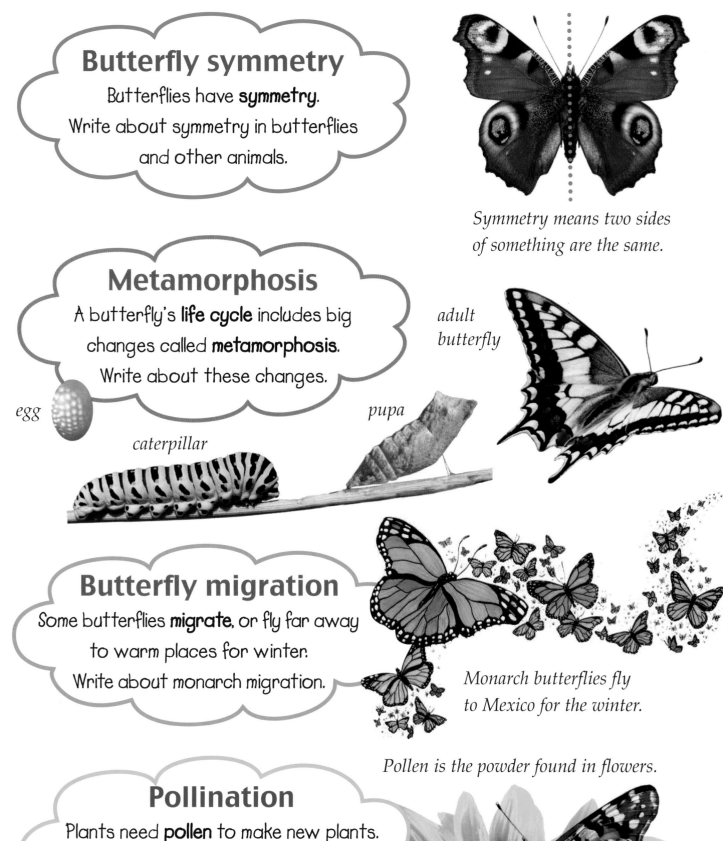

Butterfly words to know

These pages introduce the most important words that you need to know about butterflies. You can use these explanations and definitions to create a word glossary or picture glossary at the end of your own book.

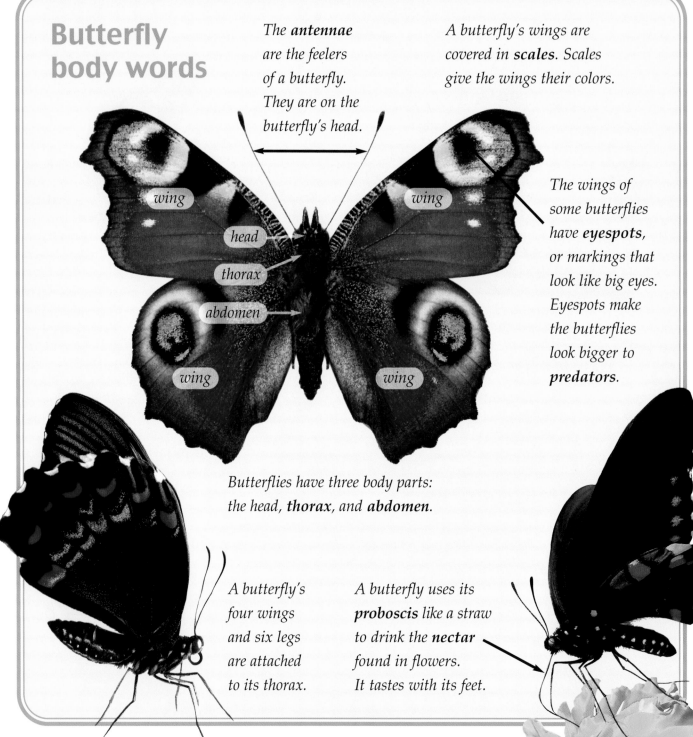

Butterfly body words

The **antennae** are the feelers of a butterfly. They are on the butterfly's head.

A butterfly's wings are covered in **scales**. Scales give the wings their colors.

The wings of some butterflies have **eyespots**, or markings that look like big eyes. Eyespots make the butterflies look bigger to **predators**.

wing

wing

head

thorax

abdomen

wing

wing

Butterflies have three body parts: the head, **thorax**, and **abdomen**.

A butterfly's four wings and six legs are attached to its thorax.

A butterfly uses its **proboscis** like a straw to drink the **nectar** found in flowers. It tastes with its feet.

Caterpillar body words

prolegs

*A caterpillar finds its way using feelers called **tentacles**.*

real legs

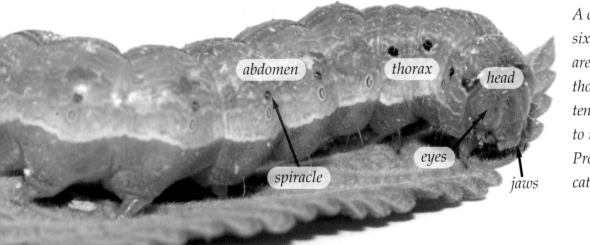

abdomen

thorax

head

eyes

jaws

spiracle

A caterpillar has six **real legs**, which are attached to its thorax. It also has ten **prolegs** attached to its abdomen. Prolegs help a caterpillar climb.

*A caterpillar breathes through tiny holes called **spiracles**.*

Some caterpillars have an **osmeterium**, which looks like soft orange horns. The osmeterium smells very bad. The smell warns predators that the caterpillar will taste bad, too. Predators are animals that hunt and eat other animals.

11

Life cycle words

A life cycle is the series of changes an animal goes through from the time it is an egg to the time it becomes an adult. A butterfly's life cycle includes big changes called metamorphosis. The metamorphosis of a butterfly has four parts: egg, caterpillar, **pupa**, and adult. The pictures on this page show the metamorphosis of a monarch butterfly.

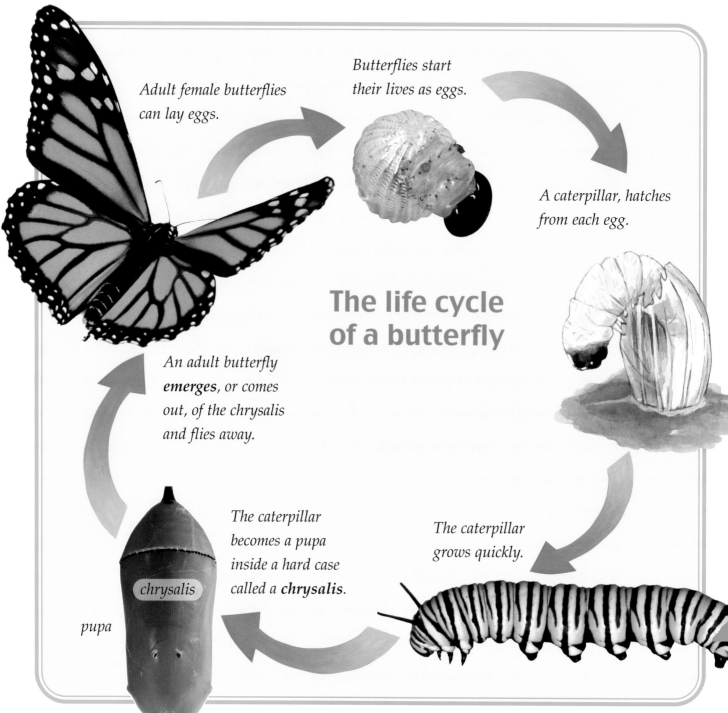

Adult female butterflies can lay eggs.

Butterflies start their lives as eggs.

A caterpillar, hatches from each egg.

The life cycle of a butterfly

An adult butterfly **emerges**, or comes out, of the chrysalis and flies away.

The caterpillar grows quickly.

The caterpillar becomes a pupa inside a hard case called a **chrysalis**.

chrysalis

pupa

Really big changes!

Most caterpillars do not look anything like the butterflies they become. The monarch butterfly on the opposite page is orange and black, but as a caterpillar, its stripes are white, yellow, and black. Look at the other butterflies on this page to see the big changes they go through during metamorphosis.

swallowtail caterpillar

pupa

swallowtail butterflies

peacock caterpillar

pupa

peacock butterflies

Did you know?

Did you know that when a caterpillar becomes a pupa, most of its body turns to mush inside the chrysalis? The body of the new butterfly, as well as its beautiful wings, are made from that mush. Write a story about what this butterfly is telling the caterpillar about metamorphosis.

Getting started

Now that you have learned some facts about caterpillars and butterflies, you can start planning your book. Read the questions below and write your answers and thoughts in a "writer's notebook." Use the notebook to record any information or ideas.

Questions to ask

- What do I already know about butterflies?
- What interests me the most about butterflies?
- Which big ideas on pages 8–9 would I like to write about?
- How will I make my book look good?
- How will I find all the information I need?

Write down ways to make your book fun, such as including art, activities, and photographs.

Looking at butterflies

Butterflies live in most parts of the world. Wherever there are a lot of flowers, there are usually butterflies. You have probably seen them in your back yard. You can also see butterflies at butterfly gardens and **conservatories**. A conservatory is a room with a glass roof and walls. There may be one near your home. At a butterfly conservatory, you can see butterflies go through metamorphosis.

*Look at a butterfly close up. What do you see? Write your **observations** in your notebook.*

Start with art!

Draw pictures of butterflies for your book. Drawing pictures will get you excited about writing your book. It will also make your book look beautiful.

Bobbie's tip

Before I start writing a book, I look for the pictures that I will need. Finding great photographs and having artists create art for my book helps me "see" how the whole book will look. The pictures inspire me and make writing easier and more fun.

Doing research

You now know a little about butterflies, but you need to **research**, or look for more facts. A great place to start is at your school or public library. Look for books on butterflies, like the ones shown on page 31. You can also find information in other books, encyclopedias, television programs, and on the Internet. Use at least two sources for your research. Take notes, but be careful not to copy someone else's work word for word. Read and understand the information and then rewrite it in your own words.

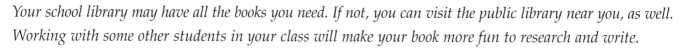

Your school library may have all the books you need. If not, you can visit the public library near you, as well. Working with some other students in your class will make your book more fun to research and write.

Watching videos of butterfly life cycles on the Internet is almost as good as watching them live. You can see a butterfly change from an egg to a caterpillar, to a pupa, and finally, to an adult butterfly. The changes happen right before your eyes! Ask your teacher to help you find the right websites.

Research review

- Write research information in your own words.
- Use at least two research sources.
- Include your own experiences with butterflies.
- Write a story about how you felt when you saw butterflies in your garden.

Take photographs of butterflies you see near your home.

Use the photographs in your butterfly book.

Ready to write!

Now that you have done some research, it is time to start writing the **body** of your book. The body of the book contains the information you have learned and want to share with others.

What is a spread?

You will find writing a book easier if you organize your ideas into short chapters called **spreads**. A spread is two pages that face each other. Each spread contains one main idea or subject. A **heading** tells you what the spread is about.

Smaller subheadings

A spread usually has several paragraphs. Each paragraph contains one topic that is part of the subject of the spread. The **subheading**, or smaller heading, tells you what a paragraph is about. What is the heading of this chapter? What are some subheadings on this spread?

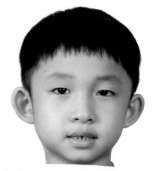

It is now time to make my **outline**! My outline is a list of the topics I will write about. The next page shows some outlines.

Bobbie's tip

In all my books, I cover one main idea on each two-page spread. When you set up your book this way, your information, ideas, and pictures are much easier to organize. The picture at the bottom of page 19 shows a spread. This book is also written in spreads.

Making an outline

Make an outline of the topics you plan to write about. Your outline will later become your table of contents. Choose the topics you will write about from the sample outlines below or add your own topics.

Body topics
What is an insect?
Caterpillar body parts
Butterfly body parts
How do butterflies eat?
A butterfly's senses
Butterfly symmetry
Butterfly wings
Butterfly art

Life cycle topics
What is a life cycle?
Hatching from eggs
Hungry caterpillars
Growing out of their skin
Finding a place to hang
Inside the chrysalis
A butterfly comes out!
Flying away

Other topics
Butterfly pollinators
Monarch migration
Butterfly habitats
Endangered butterflies
Helping butterflies
Fun with butterflies
Butterfly camouflage
Butterflies and moths

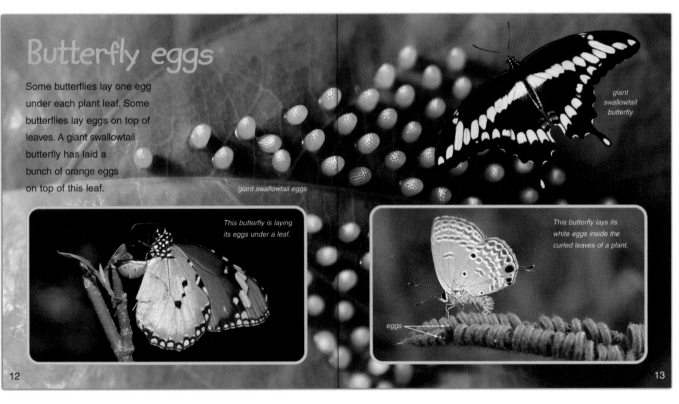

Butterfly eggs

Some butterflies lay one egg under each plant leaf. Some butterflies lay eggs on top of leaves. A giant swallowtail butterfly has laid a bunch of orange eggs on top of this leaf.

giant swallowtail eggs

giant swallowtail butterfly

This butterfly is laying its eggs under a leaf.

This butterfly lays its white eggs inside the curled leaves of a plant.

eggs

12

13

This spread appears in the book Caterpillars to Butterflies, *shown on page 31.*

Typed or written words?

Try using different **fonts** if you are writing your book on a computer. A font is a style of type. If you are writing your book by hand, you can use colors and different ways of writing that look like words typed on a computer.

What is a font?

Most of this book is written in a **plain text** font, but there are other kinds of fonts, as well. Words written in a **boldface**, or thick black, font are words that may be new to the readers. They may be explained on the page or defined in the glossary. The headings and subheadings are written in a different font than the rest of the book to make them stand out. Headings are also larger and may be in color. Choose colors that match the pictures on the pages.

Captions and fact boxes

Information about a picture is found in a **caption**. The captions in this book are written in *italics*. Letters in italics slant to the right and are smaller than plain text. **Fact boxes** bring attention to special information, ask questions, or give instructions. There are several fact boxes in this book. They look like notebook pages, such as the one shown above right.

Typing or writing?

- If you are writing your book on a computer, try using different fonts.
- Choose a plain text font that is easy to read.
- Choose heading fonts that suit your subject.
- If you are writing your book by hand, use a thick pencil, pen, or marker to make **boldfaced** words.
- Make captions smaller and *slant* your words to look like an *italic* font.
- For headings, use markers or colored pencils.

Write some captions

Write captions for these two pictures.
Use your imagination!
(top) How did the green frogs
become tongue-tied?
(bottom) How do butterflies help
flowers make fruit, seeds,
and new plants?

Font review

Plain text font is used
to write most of the
information in the book.

**Boldface font is used to
introduce new words.**

*Italic font is used
for writing captions.
A caption tells what is
happening in a picture.*

This font is used in
fact boxes that give
you extra information
or special directions.

Chapter headings are in large colored type.

**Subheadings
are smaller than
chapter headings.
They can also
be in color.**

Different ways to write

To make your book more exciting to read, you could try writing some parts in different ways. Most of this book is written as **informational** text. Informational text gives information. Parts of this book are also written in **instructional** text. Instructional text gives directions on how to do something, like write a book. Try using all the text styles shown on these two pages.

Instructional text

Read the text below, which gives instructions about how to raise a monarch butterfly in a jar. The action words are in boldface and tell you what to do. Use instructional text to write your own instructions for a butterfly activity.

Steps 1–5

Step 6

Step 7

Steps 8–9

Step 10

How to raise a monarch

1. **Cover** the inside bottom of a large jar with small stones.
2. **Find** a milkweed leaf with a caterpillar on it and put it into the jar.
3. **Add** a twig. **Cover** the top of the jar with cheesecloth. **Put** a rubber band around the cloth to hold it in place.
4. **Place** the jar in a warm but shady spot.
5. **Replace** the milkweed leaves in the jar every day. Caterpillars eat a lot!
6. **Watch** the caterpillar molt, or shed its skin, four times. It will then be ready to become a pupa and hang from the stick.
7. **Note** how the pupa changes inside as the chrysalis becomes see-through.
8. **Observe** the butterfly as it emerges from the chrysalis.
9. **Remove** the cloth from the jar.
10. **Do not touch** the butterfly.
11. **Allow** the butterfly to fly away.

Narrative text

Narrative text is written in story form. The boy in this picture is planning to catch butterflies, but when he sees a monarch flying over some yellow flowers, he is amazed by its beauty. Will he catch the butterfly? Will he watch it fly from flower to flower? Write a story about what you would do if you were this boy.

Descriptive text

Descriptive text describes a place or thing using the five **senses** of sight, hearing, smell, taste, and touch. This girl is in a garden with bushes and flowers around her. A tiger longwing butterfly has landed on her finger. How do its legs **feel** against her skin? What patterns does she **see** on the butterfly's wings? What does she **smell** in the garden? What sounds might she **hear**? How does she imagine that nectar, the butterfly's food, might **taste**? Would it taste like honey? Pretend you are this girl and write a descriptive paragraph about butterflies.

Revising your book

Once you have written your **draft**, or first try at writing your book, it is time to read it to yourself. While reading, ask yourself these questions:

- How does my writing sound to me?
- Have I included all the information I needed to include?
- Have I written about my own observations or experiences with butterflies?
- Have I used different writing styles in my book?
- Do my captions give interesting information and describe what is happening in the pictures?
- Do my sentences make sense?
- Did I use **comparisons**?
- Do my questions make my readers think?
- How can I **revise**, or rewrite, my book to make it better?

How can I make my book better? What changes do I need to make?

Ask your teacher to read through your book and suggest some changes you could make.

Share your draft

After you have read your draft and made some changes, it is time to share it with others. It is important to listen to what others say about your writing. If someone does not understand the information the way you have written it, your readers will not understand your book, either.

- What did the listeners not understand?
- What questions did they ask?
- What suggestions did they make?

Bobbie revises

Don't worry about making mistakes. Every author revises his or her books. I revise each book several times, and my **editors** make even more changes! Editors read a draft, check facts, and rewrite parts of it to make it sound better. You can read about how to **edit** and **proofread** your book on pages 26–27.

Editing and proofreading

Editing is making sure that your writing is clear and correct. After you have revised your writing, you may still find parts of your book that you could have written more clearly. You may want to use some new words that are longer and more interesting than the ones you used, such as "transformed" instead of "changed." Proofreading is checking for errors such as spelling mistakes, capital letters, **punctuation**, and sentence structure.

*A **thesaurus** will help you find several **synonyms** for each word. A synonym is a word that means the same as another word.*

Editing checklist

• Have you covered all the information you intended to cover?

• Have you used new and interesting words?

• Have you used the correct words? If you are not sure, look them up in a dictionary.

• Do your subheadings introduce the information in your paragraphs?

• Have you used different kinds of sentences?

Proofreading checklist

- Are your sentences complete?
- Have you used the correct punctuation?
- Have you capitalized names and the first words in sentences?
- Have you spelled names and other words correctly?

Questions to ask

There are many questions in this book. Some are questions we ask. Others are questions you ask yourself. How do questions help you?

- They help you review the work you have done and what you still need to cover.
- They help you think of new ideas to include in your book.
- Write some questions starting with what, when, who, where, why, or how.

Designing your book

Designing is planning how your book will look so that people will want to read it. Writing text in a certain way, such as in fact boxes, is part of design. Using different fonts and colors also makes the book more attractive to readers.

Diagrams with captions

The other very important part is putting different kinds of pictures into your book. **Diagrams**, for example, show parts of something. The diagrams on pages 10–11 have labels and captions on and around the body parts of the caterpillars and butterflies. The diagrams on pages 12–13 use arrows to show the steps in butterfly life cycles.

These three butterfly diagrams show symmetry. Both sides of the butterflies are the same.

Making pages look good

Different kinds of pictures and text make the reader want to learn more. You can draw and paint your own pictures of caterpillars and butterflies or download photos from the Internet. Ask a parent or teacher to help you find pictures that are free to use. Print these pictures and put them into your book. Look at the design of each spread in this book to give you more good ideas about how to design your book.

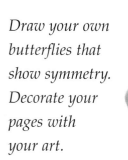

Draw your own butterflies that show symmetry. Decorate your pages with your art.

Draw one big picture on a page or several smaller ones. Decorate your pages with colorful caterpillars, butterflies, and flowers.

Use photographs that you have taken or ones that were taken of you with a caterpillar or butterfly.

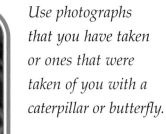

About the author
Write something interesting about yourself and tell why readers will like your book.

The life cycle of a butterfly

Your name

The life cycle of a butterfly

Your name

Above is an example of a front and back cover. You can draw your own cover pictures or download them. Your title page will look similar to your cover. Draw different pictures or use the cover pictures.

Finishing up

Publishing your book is the last step. If you wrote your book on the computer, you could make an eBook that many students could enjoy. Before you publish your book on the computer or by hand, you will need to complete all the parts of the book mentioned on pages 6 and 7—the copyright page, table of contents, glossary, and index. Find these pages in this book. They can act as guides when you make your own pages.

Copyright page

Your copyright page will include the names of all the people who helped you with your book, the books you used for research, and the sources for pictures you downloaded. This page may also include a dedication. To whom will you dedicate your book?

Table of contents

Your table of contents is a list of the headings of all the spreads you wrote. The page numbers can be placed at the left or right of the headings. (See page 3.)

Glossary

Make a picture dictionary or word glossary and put it at the end of your book. Define special words about butterflies that your readers may not know. Sort the glossary in ABC order.

Index

The index is a list of the topics in a book. It is also in ABC order and gives the page numbers of where the topics can be found (see the index on page 32 of this book).

Books to read

The books shown here were written by me, Bobbie Kalman. They will help you write your book about butterflies. Find them in your school or public library.

Caterpillars to Butterflies
Bobbie Kalman

Looking at nature
What is Symmetry in nature?
Bobbie Kalman

The Life Cycle of a Butterfly
A Bobbie Kalman Book

Endangered Butterflies
A Bobbie Kalman Book

Insect Bodies
A Bobbie Kalman Book

What is pollination?
Bobbie Kalman

Metamorphosis Changing Bodies
A Bobbie Kalman Book

Glossary

Note: Some boldfaced words are defined where they appear in the book.

comparison The act of determining the likenesses and differences in an object or event

descriptive A writing style that uses the five senses of sight, hearing, smell, taste, and touch

diagram An illustration or photograph with labels that show the parts of something

editor Someone who checks facts and grammar in someone's writing and rewrites parts when necessary

informational A writing style that gives information about something

instructional A writing style that gives instructions or directions on how to do something

metamorphosis The total change of an animal's body from one form to another

narrative A writing style that tells something in story form

nectar A sweet liquid in flowers

observation The act of seeing or noticing something

publisher A person or company that is responsible for printing and distributing a written book

punctuation The use of marks, such as periods or commas, to make the meaning of a sentence clear

Index